Copyright

Unlock Your Child's FULL Potential

Advance Praise

Making a positive difference every day !

Thanks to all my FUNDA team past and present for helping me engage, inspire motivate and empower children to get active, learn, have fun and reach their full potential at home, school and in life.

Thanks to all our FUNDA partnering schools, supporting teachers. A special mention to our FUNDA loving children and families.

You mean the world to me, you make my heart sing ...

Dedication

Be Yourself – No Matter What!

–––––––––––––––––––––

To Rachel the love of my life, you are my Rock.

To my growing boys; Theo & Louie:

I love you to the moon and back.

You inspire me,
You challenge me,
You make me laugh,
You make me grow,
You are my biggest why.

Being your Dad is the GREATEST
adventure on planet earth.

You all mean the world to me.

Hi, my name is Kieran, I'm the founder of FUNDA.

I struggled whilst attending school. I was an active learner and a destructive participant in the classroom. Children used to make fun of me for not being able to do basic things they could.

I was, however, good at one thing, playing sport, especially football. It was the only thing that could keep my attention and focus, so much so that I wanted to become a professional footballer. Like so many children this was my big dream.

I came so close to achieving my dream, until one night I had a near fatal car crash, that was a turning point in my life. I made the decision to turn to education, learning, coaching and teaching children.

I woke up one night with one of those lightbulb moments and that's when the FUNDA brand was born. Inspiring and motivating children to get active, learn, grow and have fun. I want to help children realise that they can be anything they want to be in life if they truly believe in themselves, work hard and develop the ultimate growth mindset, resilience, self-confidence and positive attitude.

I have been blessed to have been recognised for my work, as a multi-award winning company and Entrepreneur of the Year. FUNDA's even been officially recognised by Her Majesty the Queen, who said;

"Keep Up The Excellent Work And Efforts With What You Deliver To Children And Our Communities. I look Forward To Meeting You Once Again In The Near Future".
(Her Majesty The Queen Of England)

My mission is to engage, inspire, motivate and empower children worldwide supporting their Physical Education, Health, Wellbeing and Personal Development. I want to motivate millions of children to access these engaging learning materials, resources, activities and the 'FUNDA WAY' curriculum so they can live life to their fullest and unlock their full potential.

You can access lots of Free resources, activities and support online anytime, anywhere by visiting www.FUNDAgreatness.com

Best regards

Coach Kieran

When you hide your voice, you rob the world of your creativity.

Unlock Your Full Potential

 Physical Activity

 Role Model

 Critical Thinking

 Rewards

 Progress

 Communication

 Manners

 Creative Thinking

 Focus

 Fine Motor Skills

 Mindset

 Hygiene

 Fitness

 Health

 Self Confidence

 Problem Solving

 Mindfulness

 Leadership

 Skills

 Inspiration

» Free Online Access

Thousands Of Education, Physical & Personal Development Resources, Activities For Kids Online

www.FUNDAgreatness.com

BOOKMARKS

I *believe* in my dreams

I *learn* from my mistakes

My ideas are unique

I *am* amazing

I *can learn* anything

I *believe* in myself

I *can* make good choices

I *always* try my best

Funda

_____

Journey Starts Here

What do I want to Improve on?

Write or Draw below.

Through This Journey You Will Learn...

What Growth Mindset is...

How to perform Fundamentals

Nutrition for a healthy lifestyle

All about day to day life

Gross & Fine Motor Skills

Additional FUN break away activities

This Is Me

Draw yourself below

You don't have to be PERFECT to be AMAZING

Funda

GROWTH MINDSET
VS FIXED MINDSET

Read all the mindset statements on the next page, cut them out,
then sort into the correct column.

Growth Mindset	Fixed Mindset
In a growth mindset, people believe that their most basic abilities can be developed through dedication and hard work.	Believing that your qualities are fixed traits and you can't change what you think and also that people are either born smart or not smart.

I'm never going to understand this.

I am so good at this.

I GIVE UP!

This will be challenging but I'll keep going.

I should try a different strategy.

This is too hard.

I'll never be as smart as them.

I'm on the right track.

I'm going to have to think through this one more time.

I am working really hard at this.

I've never been good at this anyway.

I wasn't born to be smart

I will keep TRYING!

I believe I will achieve my goals.

I can't do this YET

Tomorrow I will get a fresh look at this.

Threading Activity

STEP 1
Get a piece of card

STEP 2
Hole punch the piece of card in different places.

STEP 3
Make a cylinder shape with your card and glue or staple it together

GLUE

STEP 4
Give your child the pipe cleaners to put through the holes you made. This will develop their fine motor skills.

What do you need?

1x Piece of card

10 Pipe Cleaners

A hole punch

A stapler

Sock Toss

UNDERARM

OVERARM

- Set 2 targets 1 on the floor and 1 stood.

- This could be a hoop (floor) toilet roll tube (stood)

- Get lots of rolled up socks (these are generally a good size for your hand)

- Try to land in the hoop with an underarm throw and knock over the tube with an overarm throw.

- Challenge friends or family to see who can do it in the fewest shots.

> TopTip – Move all breakable items!

Gratitude Spot

A Gratitude spot is a spot you stand on when you want to say what you're Thankful and Grateful for.

We would suggest that you use your spot before bed.

And when you wake up to start your day off right.

You can pick between a blue or pink spot or you can design your own.

My Spot

My Spot

My Spot

My Spot

My Spot

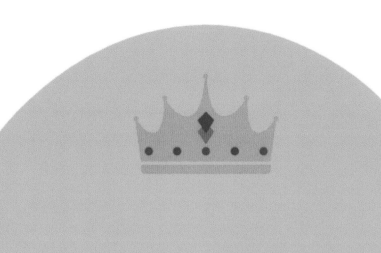

My Spot

"Why fit in when you were born to **STAND OUT?"**

-Dr. Seuss

SHOW ME HOW

 Kangaroo	 Flamingo	 Snake	 Shark
 Tiger	 Monkey	 Fish	 Dog
 Eagle	 Elephant	 Bull	 Horse

- Drop a coin/token onto the table above.

- Whichever picture it lands on, you must mimic that animal.

- Try and use big movements as well as small movements.

- Challenge friends and family to a competition. Whoever does the best animal impression wins.

Funda.

Beautiful Me

My Mirror

Write positive compliments to yourself inside the mirror. Practice picking up the mirror and reading those positive statements about yourself. Also look into a real mirror and say them to yourself with confidence.

Beautiful Me

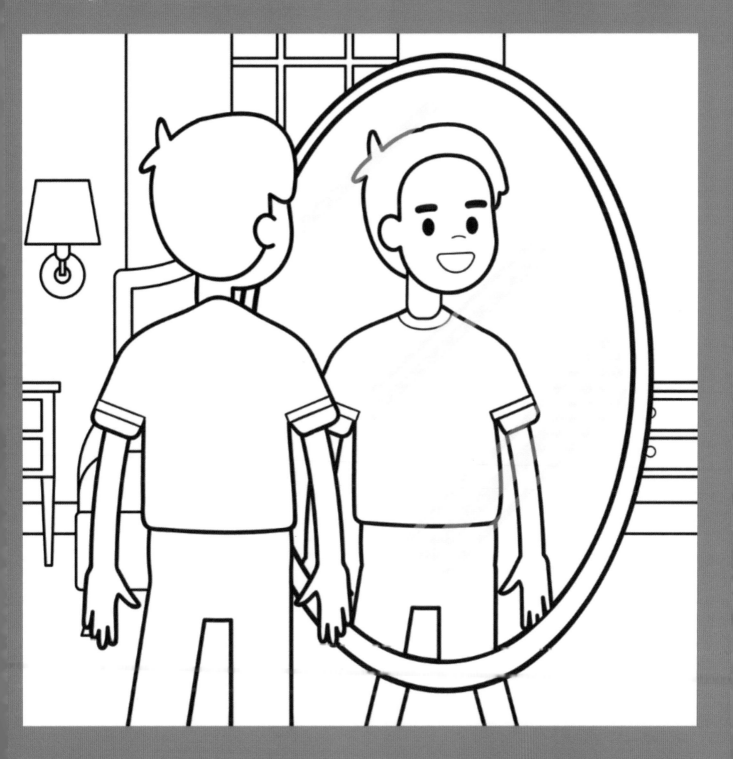

My LOVE Map

**Write or draw in the heart below
what you love about yourself.**

EAT A RAINBOW

Red, Orange, Yellow, Green and Purple

Please find fruit and veg which are these colours.

How do we keep our teeth healthy?

Write the words inside the tooth.

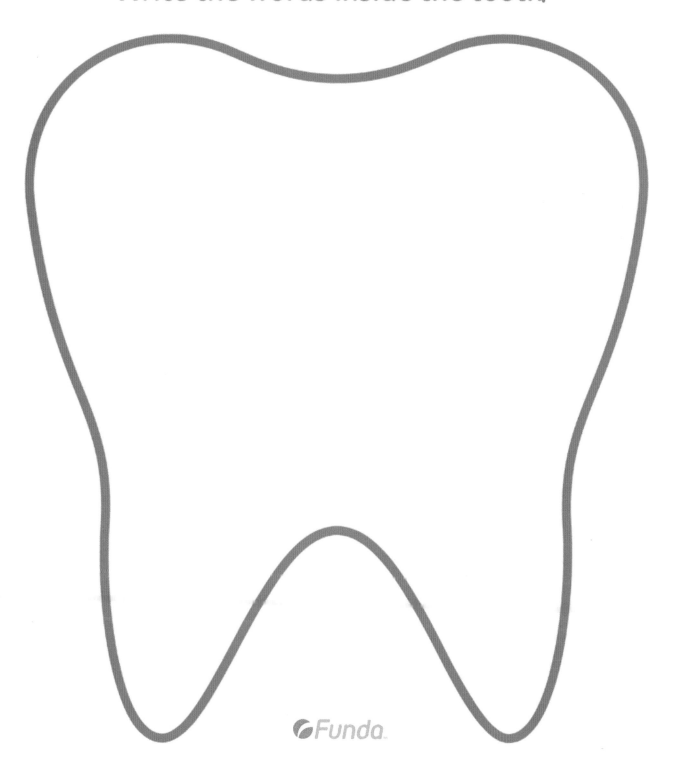

Funda

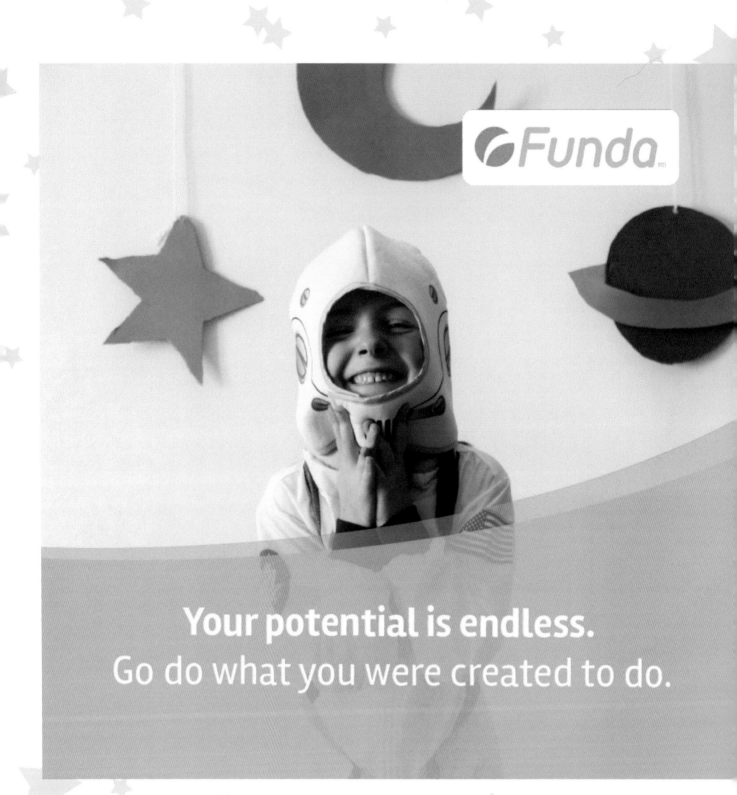

Your potential is endless.
Go do what you were created to do.

Movement Dice

Jump

Run

Reach

Balance

Crouch

Crab

Funda.

Mindset is what separates
the best from the rest.

FILL YOUR PLATE

WITH THE COLOURS

OF THE RAINBOW

WHAT PLEASES THE EYE

PLEASES THE BODY

How to
BRUSH YOUR TEETH

Step 1

I get my toothbrush and toothpaste

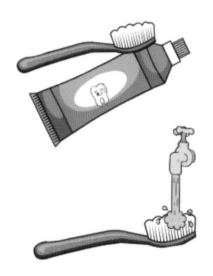

Step 2

I'll get my toothbrush wet before I put the toothpaste on

Step 3

I'll put the toothpaste on my toothbrush

Step 4

Then brush all your teeth for 2 minutes

Step 5

Rinse your mouth with water

Funda

Things I love about me

Write In the hearts below what you love about yourself.

GOOD FOR MY TEETH

BAD FOR MY TEETH

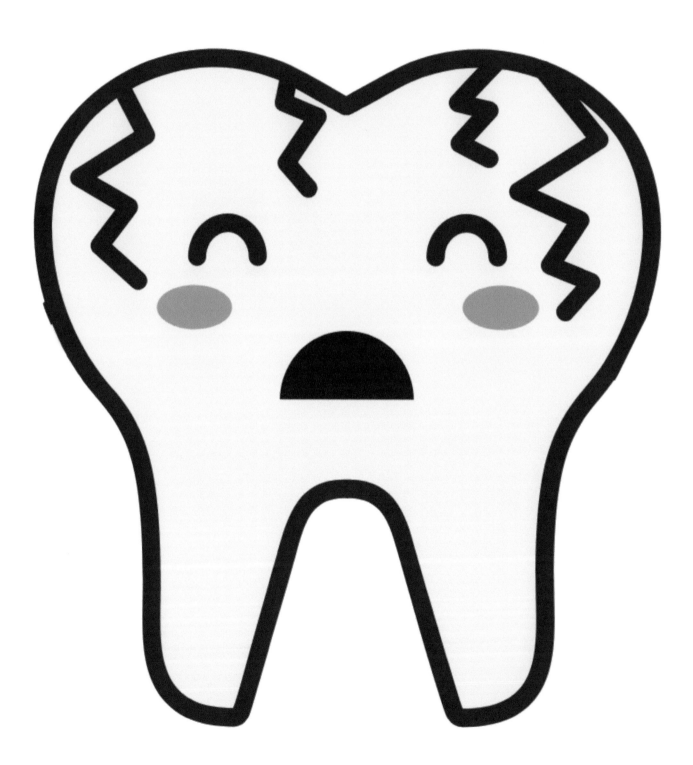

Cut out the food icons and glue them on what you think is Good for your Teeth or Bad for your Teeth.

GET UP EVERY MORNING AND TELLYOURSELF

"I CAN

DO THIS!"

Growth Mindset Word Search

```
Q T Q M T N B Q S Q Y Y S K D
C O L E P O R S N S Y T K A R
S L A O G E L A R I R K I D M
Y N E M L R R U E Y M G L I X
R E S P E C T S I L T U L F B
O P P O R T U N I T I E S F M
C E P G E N G E C S V E D E V
E V F L A G J H V O T O M R S
R W X F L C A C R E E E Y E E
O L S W O L B P C G I C N N Z
L U V S L R M L W T P L T C E
P J E E V I T A P P L M E E E
X K N R X F N P J G E O M B T
E G S E K A T S I M H C H E D
E W Q Q G O A M A M R N Y G Z
```

BELIEVE   CHALLENGE   DIFFERENCE   EFFORT   EXPLORE   GOALS
HELP   IMPROVE   LEARN   MISTAKES   OPPORTUNITIES
PERSISTENCE   RESPECT   SKILLS   TRYING   YET

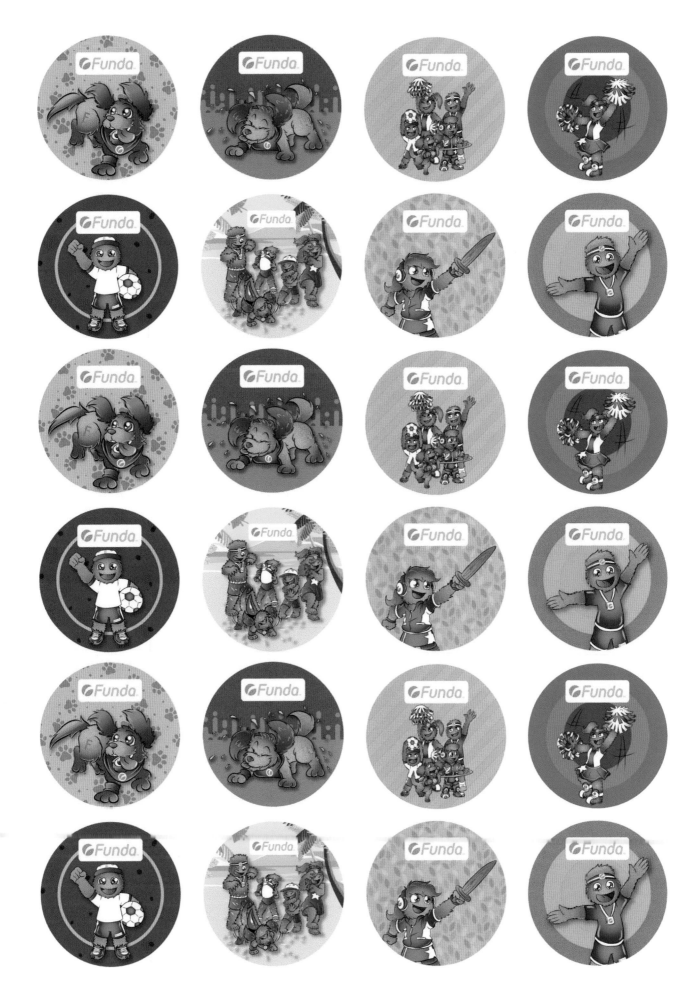

Healthy or Not

✂ Cut out the food icons on the other page and glue them onto this page. Where you think the food belongs either in the healthy section or the not healthy section.

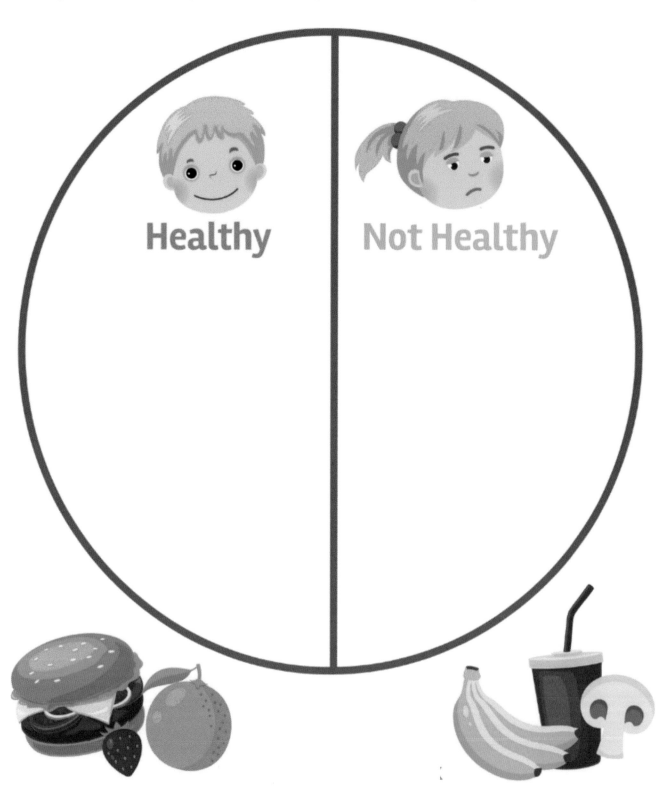

Healthy

Not Healthy

What Vegetables Do You Like The Most?

1–10

10						
9						
8						
7						
6						
5						
4						
3						
2						
1						
Vegetables >						

Draw a picture or write the name of the vegetables in the boxes above.

- When you have tried a variety of vegetables score them out of 10.
- Add your favourite vegetables to the graph above.
- Show your parents so they then know what vegetables you like the most.

Eat Like You Love Your Body.

Movement Dice

Funda

Healthy vs Unhealthy

Can you help Funda and his friends
colour in the healthy foods only?

Funda

WHERE DOES FOOD COME FROM?

Can you help Funda matching up where the foods are made/grown?
There may be more than one.

Connect the dots

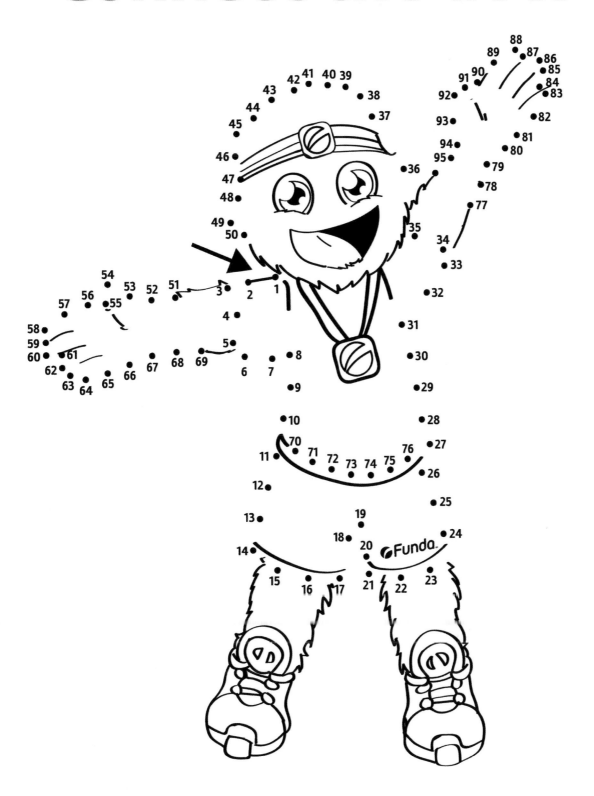

Connect the dots

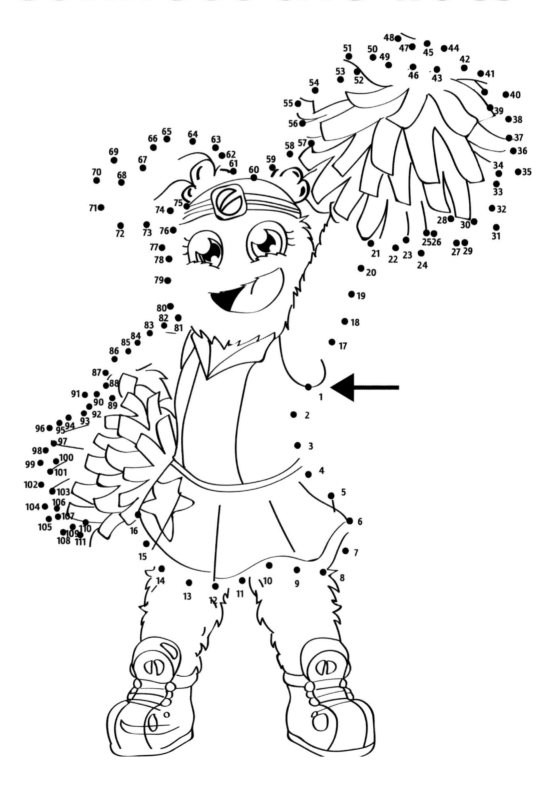

Connect the dots

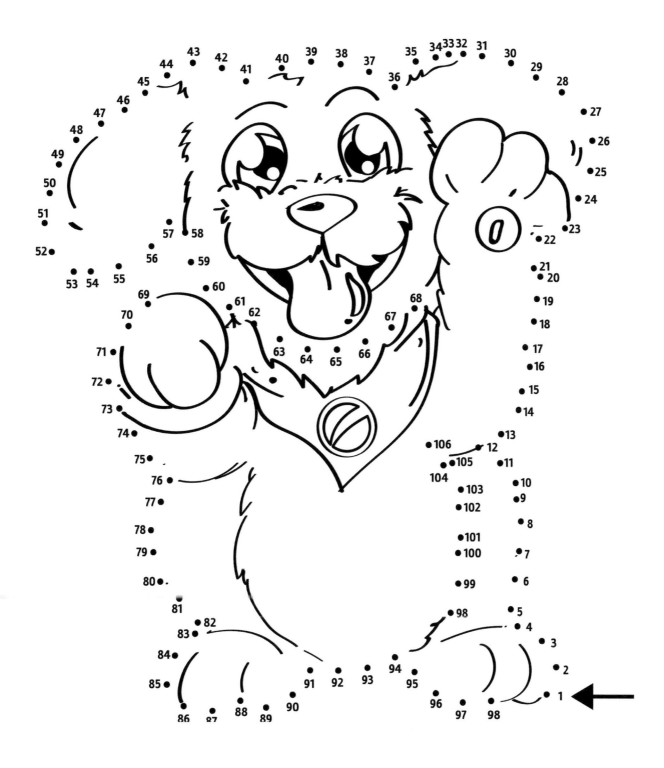

Connect the dots

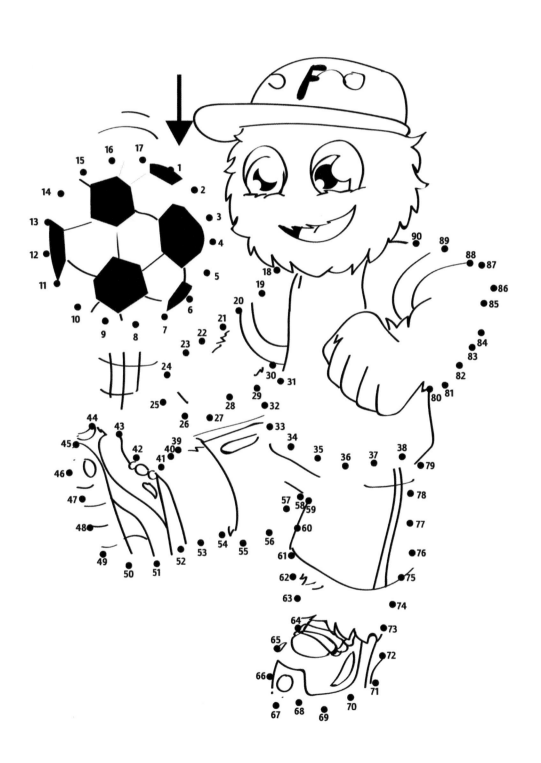

Connect the dots

STORY STARTER

I was just about to eat my apple when _____

_____

_____

_____

_____

_____

_____

_____

_____

_____

_____

**An alien visited my house the other day for dinner.
So I made healthy** _____

_____

_____

_____

_____

_____

_____

_____

_____

I went out with my friends and we found a pear tree and some blueberry bushes, so we _____

_____

_____

_____

_____

_____

_____

_____

_____

_____

I went to the market yesterday to see the
fishmonger. When I was there I decided to get
some really healthy... _____

_____

_____

_____

_____

_____

_____

_____

_____

Hide & Find Stones

This fun activity will help you practice your fine motor skills, exercise your creativity and expand your vocabulary.

Work as a alone or as a team with a friend or family member to design a stone. Draw any design on your stones, then hide them around your home , garden or anywhere outside and see who will find your stones.

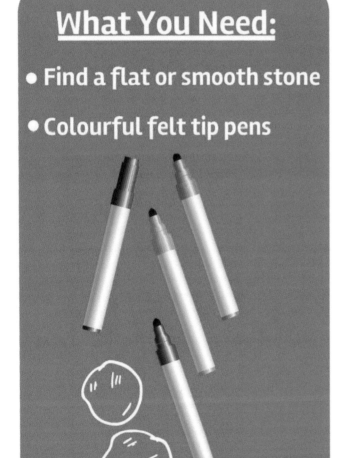

What You Need:

- Find a flat or smooth stone
- Colourful felt tip pens

1. Once you have your stones and felt tip pens in front of you ...

2. Now it's time for the FUN part where you can get as creative as you like by drawing any design onto your stone.

3. Once your stone is designed how you'd like, find a hiding place in your house or garden and hide your stone.

4. Now it's a race to see who can find the other person's stone first.

CAN YOU BALANCE LIKE
FUNDA?

Cut the spinner out below, and ask for help to push a pencil through the middle.

Spin the spinner. Whatever number it lands on try and perform a balance with only that number of body parts touching the floor.

GOOD MORNING!

TO DO		DONE!
✓	**Eat Breakfast**	◯
✓	**Brush Teeth**	◯
✓	**Get Dressed**	◯
✓	**Brush Hair**	◯
✓	**Pick Up Toys**	◯
✓	**Help Tidy Up**	◯

GOOD NIGHT!

TO DO		DONE!
◯	**Pick Up Toys**	◯
◯	**Take a bath**	◯
◯	**Brush Teeth**	◯
◯	**Put on Pajamas**	◯
◯	**Go to Toilet & Wash Hands**	◯
◯	**Bedtime Stories**	◯
◯	**Go to Sleep**	◯

TRIP WIRE

- For this activity you will need clothes pegs and lots of string

- Place clothes pegs around the room

- Tie string around the clothes pegs situated in different places

- This creates a spier–web type obstacle course

- Time how long it takes you to get through the course,
  then try and beat it

- Even better... Challenge friends and family

- You can even do this in the garden, park or outside

**TIP: Add items to the string that make noise i.e. milk bottle tops,
so you know if you touch the string or not.**

MY GROWTH MINDSET REFLECTION

Growth Mindset Behaviour	Always	Often	Not YET	How I'll improve
I can work as a team.				
I try my best to improve things.				
If I am unsuccessful at first, I'll try new ideas.				
I keep going through obstacles and challenges.				
I set goals and watch my progress.				
I take back feedback from others.				
I learn from my mistakes.				
I do not skip challenging tasks, I take them on.				
I can change my fixed mindset to growth mindset thoughts				

MY FEELINGS & ME
Journal

I feel scared when...

_____

- - - - - - - - - - - - - - - - - - - -

_____

_____

- - - - - - - - - - - - - - - - - - - -

_____

_____

- - - - - - - - - - - - - - - - - - - -

_____

_____

- - - - - - - - - - - - - - - - - - - -

_____

_____

I feel
shy
when...

_____

- - - - - - - - - - - - - - - - - - -

_____

- - - - - - - - - - - - - - - - - - -

_____

_____

- - - - - - - - - - - - - - - - - - -

_____

_____

- - - - - - - - - - - - - - - - - - -

_____

- - - - - - - - - - - - - - - - - - -

_____

I feel proud when...

_____

- -

_____

_____

- -

_____

_____

- -

_____

_____

- -

_____

I feel nervous when...

_____

- - - - - - - - - - - - - - - - - - -

_____

- - - - - - - - - - - - - - - - - - -

_____

- - - - - - - - - - - - - - - - - - -

_____

- - - - - - - - - - - - - - - - - - -

_____

- - - - - - - - - - - - - - - - - - -

_____

I feel surprised when...

_____

- -

_____

- -

_____

- -

_____

- -

_____

- -

_____

I feel excited when...

_____
- -
_____
_____
- -
_____
_____
- -
_____
_____
- -
_____

I feel confused when...

_____

- -

_____

_____

- -

_____

_____

- -

_____

_____

- -

_____

_____

- -

_____

I feel happy when...

_____

- -

_____

- -

_____

- -

_____

- -

_____

- -

_____

I feel embarrased when...

_____

- -

_____

- -

_____

- -

_____

- -

_____

- -

_____

Find & Colour

Use the colour key to colour in the picture.

Colour Key

we | when | your | can | said

A sign of a hard worker is one who **works without complaint.**

MY GOAL

_____

_____

_____

WHY I want to achieve this goal

_____

_____

I will do this first

Then I will do this

Then this

and finally this

I will achieve it by:

MY OBSTACLES

If...

My actions to overcome them:

then I will...

If...

My actions to overcome them:

then I will...

REACH
for the Stars

Write or Draw your goals on the stars on the
next page and place them below.

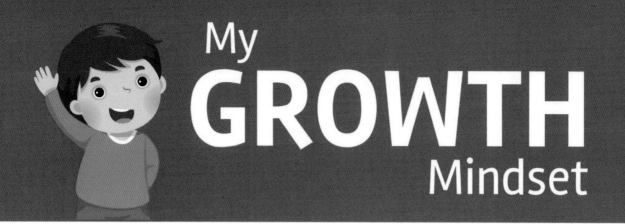

My
GROWTH
Mindset

I Can _____

I Can _____

I Can Not

_____

YET!

This is me when I learn

My Future Map

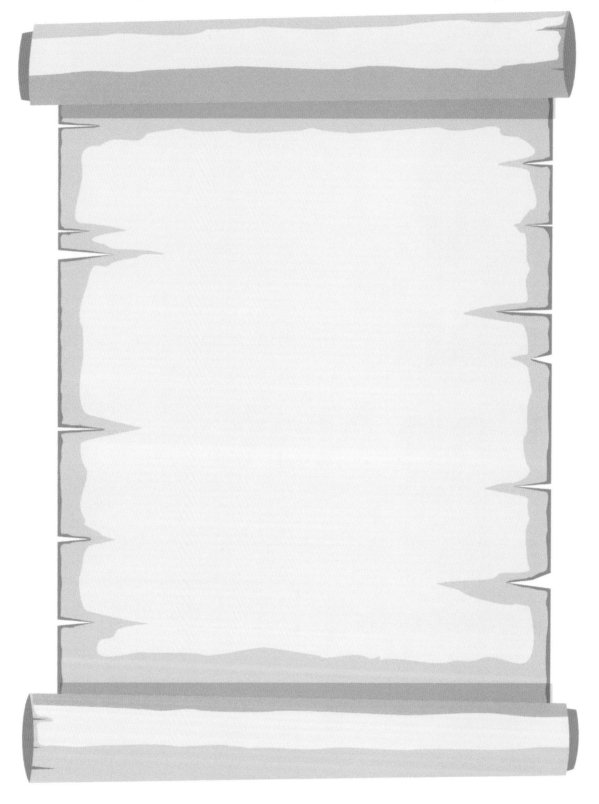

I can't YET...

Think of something that you want to learn but haven't yet. Draw below.

I haven't learned how to...

YET!

SUCCESS!

Make a PLAN of HOW you're going to learn it.

Write down the obstacles you have to take on, on each of the steps of the progress stairs starting from the bottom.

STEP 4

STEP 3

I can!

STEP 2

STEP 1

WHEN YOU FAIL, ALL YOU WANT TO DO IS GIVE UP!

When you try something new and you weren't successful
Instead of giving up what words would you keep in mind?

NEVER GIVE UP!

What Are YOU Good At?

Write it

Draw it

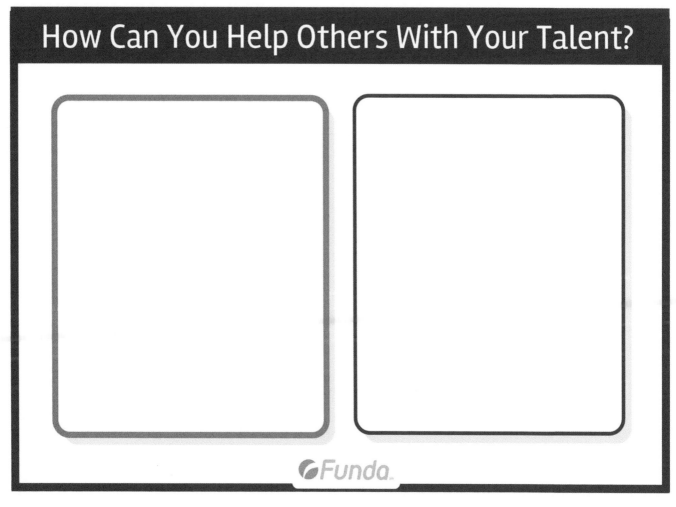

How Can You Help Others With Your Talent?

Funda

WHAT ARE YOUR RESPONSIBILITIES?

Write or draw about your responsibilities at home and at school.

AT HOME

AT SCHOOL

I CAN LEARN ANYTHING

Make **OOPS!** Mistakes

HAVE FUN!

Learn New Skills

PLAY MORE

Teach Others

Read More

Spend more time Outside

PAUSE to THINK

Explore MORE

Take on NEW Challenges

Make a Difference Every Day

WHAT ARE THE NEW THINGS YOU'D LIKE TO TRY?

What are the new things you'd like to try
Write or Draw in the shapes below.

HOW DO YOU SHOW RESPECT?

Write or draw below How You Show Respect...

TO YOUR PARENTS	**TO YOURSELF**
TO YOUR FRIENDS	**TO YOUR TEACHERS**

MY POSITIVITY JAR

Write or draw in the Jar below
Positive and Grateful thoughts.

THINK
POSITIVE

INSTEAD OF "I MESSED UP!"

Funda

I Will Try A

different

Strategy!

INSTEAD OF "I GIVE UP!"

Achieve Goals

Believe In Yourself

Challenge Yourself

Develop Skills

show Effort

learn from Failure

Good Mistakes

Help Others

keep Improving

Just be Yourself

Keep Trying

Learn New Things

Make A Difference

Never Give Up

new Opportunities

Persistence

ask Questions

Respect Others

Set Goals

Team Work

be Unique

be Valiant

Work Hard

eXplore

'not Yet'

be Zealous

Funda

"Becoming is better than being"

– CAROL DWECK

"Anyone who has never made a mistake has never tried anything new"

— ALBERT EINSTEIN

"A diamond is chunk of coal that did well under pressure"

– HENRY KISSENGER

Colour in the FUNDA Family

Learn Your Colours

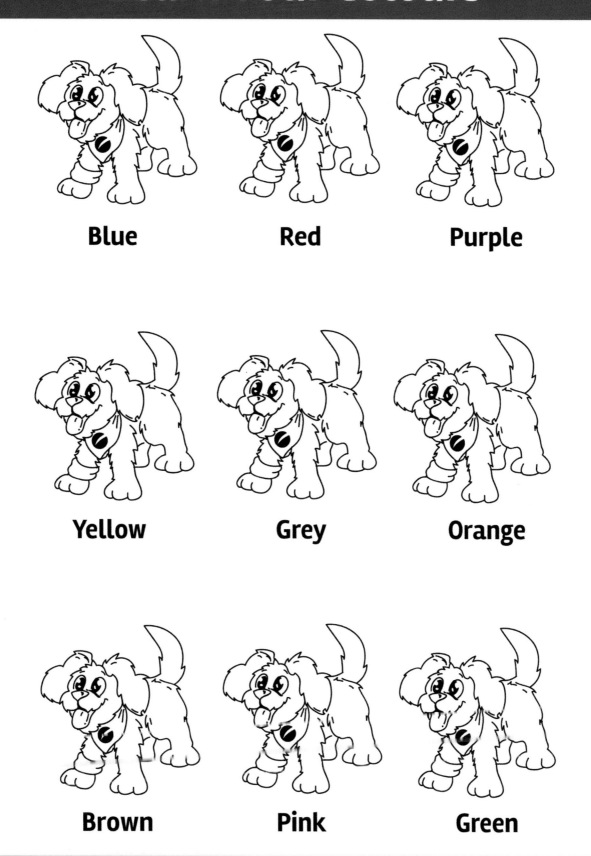

Blue   Red   Purple

Yellow   Grey   Orange

Brown   Pink   Green

My Acts Of
Kindness

On the next page, you will find different shapes that you can draw or write your acts of kindness on.
Cut out and Stick the shapes onto this page.

Where's the Funda Family On the Seaside?

This may take some

Time
AND
Effort

INSTEAD OF
"THIS IS TOO HARD!"

WORD SEARCH

P	A	E	N	S	F	F	E	D	P
A	V	J	X	N	B	R	F	M	W
S	I	I	I	L	N	I	M	O	C
S	R	V	N	L	L	E	Y	T	I
I	E	Y	S	V	E	N	F	I	D
O	S	G	P	Y	A	D	D	V	S
N	P	S	I	X	R	L	F	A	M
A	E	Y	R	R	N	Y	U	T	O
T	C	R	E	A	T	E	L	E	P
E	T	R	U	S	T	F	T	A	E

WORDS TO FIND:

MOTIVATE   INSPIRE   VALUE   FRIENDLY

PASSIONATE   CREATE   TRUST   LEARN   RESPECT

What am I MISSING?

INSTEAD OF
"I'M NOT GOOD AT THIS"

Build and Colour in your own
FUNDETTE FUNDA Character

Funda

Practice Sheet

Aa Bb Cc Dd Ee Ff
Gg Hh Ii Jj Kk Ll Mm
Nn Oo Pp Qq Rr Ss Tt
Uu Vv Ww Xx Yy Zz

Aa Bb Cc Dd Ee Ff
Gg Hh Ii Jj Kk Ll Mm
Nn Oo Pp Qq Rr Ss Tt
Uu Vv Ww Xx Yy Zz

FIND THE FOOD

Find the foods listed below. Circle the healthy foods in one colour and the unhealthy foods in a different colour.

```
                    B L E
                T U M L C L Z K J
            Z O A R E Y R P T P Q E E
        N L M Z Z H E E C P J K C S Y B B
      E Q A W A Z O E Z J A X Y J S B W U E
    C D T I Y T I N B K D M H B C C W A T K R
    H O B N H B P C E Y G H Y F E O S E T C U
  I O P W V U       Y P O T L       W I E C F N
  A C W S N X       F T X O G       V G R T M B
E K O X A H H K M Y D W O M C R R V S Z H O S D U
X K L A X J X V L O V R Q B J X B P G L O W U X Y
C R A Z Q N F G G V U A M C O H Y M T R S A R R G
I T H T C B F U C B V P R E T A W H Q H O F V P V H Q
D E S E O F H N L A P O T A T O C M S P T R F K U K Y
X H O U A L F X B B A U Q M N B G U B A C J R J R K G
G C B O   V M K E G D G A K C M H I Y V   V A M Y
Z N Z Q   P E K A Z Y D Y S B K Y H   S N C O
A K F R J   D S M D W D Y C H C G   P L H U C
X S W Z L                         S C D Y M
S X K D K Y                     I P T J E J
    A B R O C C O L I X J B V V D R V V A D G
    Y L A O Y F M R R I U P Z L C H W O Q U H
    S D A N M W M G R B L M D A V S B S Q
    W W I H C X G P I N E A P P L E C
      Q N O E V L L Z K P N J F
          R N J D C C U I M
              F K G
```

APPLE	BROCCOLI	BURGER
BUTTER	CAKE	CARROT
CHOCOLATE	CRISPS	HOTDOG
KEBAB	MUSHROOM	PINEAPPLE
PIZZA	POTATO	SWEETS
TOMATO	WATER	

ODD ONE OUT

1. Write in the box below the image what the food/drink is.
2. CUT THE CARDS OUT BELOW; Pick one at random and guess the odd one out!
   Continue until you have guessed all cards.

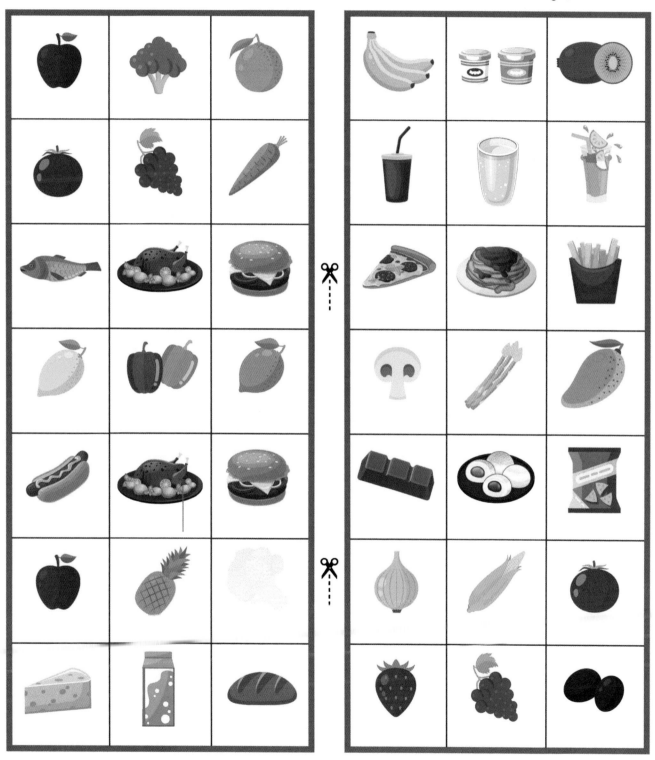

TRAFFIC LIGHT LUNCHBOX

This is great tool to make sure your lunchbox is healthy. Have a look and put your favourite foods in the colours. Is your favourite lunch healthy?

RED — Rarely include these.

- Chocolate
- Crisps
- High Sugar Snacks
- Cereal bars
- Cereals
- Fruit Jellies
- Sweets
- Energy/Fizzy drinks
- Children's yoghurt
- Savoury Crackers
- Flavoured Milk

AMBER — Can be included in smaller amounts.

- Cheese
- Cold meats
- Yoghurt (Natural)
- Rice Cakes
- Milk
- Fish
- Light Mayo
- White bread
- Healthy Sandwich Filling

GREEN — Include as many as you like of these.

- Fruit (Dried or Fresh)
- Veg sticks
- Water
- Brown bread
- Pasta
- Salad
- Home made cereal bars

DAILY FOOD PYRAMID

RARELY

2 SERVINGS

3 SERVINGS

5+ SERVINGS

6+ SERVINGS

Remember the...

YET

I can't do this... YET

I don't know... YET

This doesn't work... YET

I don't get it... YET

It doesn't make sense... YET

I'm not good at this... YET

Good ways to be a
FRIEND

Write or draw how someone could be a good friend

Bad ways to be a
FRIEND

Write or draw how someone could be a bad friend

Things I can't do
YET...

Write or draw below the things you can't do YET...

Learning Time With FUNDA

Draw the hands on each clock to match the time given.

11:30	**10:35**	**8:00**	**12:10**
7:35	**2:55**	**3:10**	**4:15**
8:55	**6:30**	**7:50**	**5:15**

MY ROLE MODEL

A role model is someone that you look up to and admire. They are someone that has certain qualities, behaviors, or relationships that you hope to have as well. Draw a picture of your role model and answer the questions below!

NAME

What positive qualities does this person have?

_____

_____

What do you admire most about them?

_____

_____

How have they inspired you?

_____

_____

In what ways are YOU a role model?

_____

_____

I CAN BE A ROLE MODEL!

Directions: Draw a picture of how you can be a role model in the following places.

CLASSROOM

PLAYGROUND

COMMUNITY

TODAY I CAN

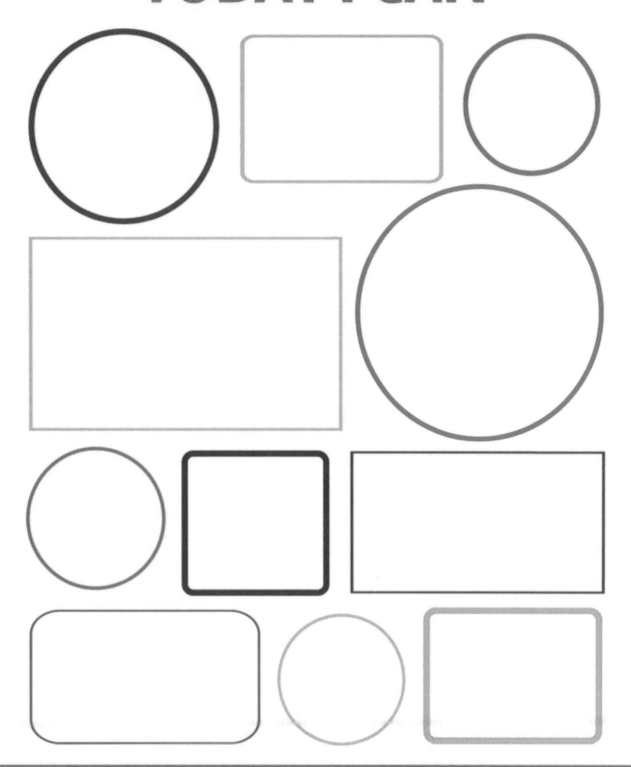

BUT TOMORROW ANYTHING IS POSSIBLE

"This is your time to be creative"

Funda

WASH YOUR HANDS!

Before touching babies

Before eating food

After blowing your nose, coughing or sneezing

After handling rubbish

After playing outside

After using the toilet

After touching animals

7 THINGS THAT I LIKE ABOUT MYSELF...

1 _____

2 _____

3 _____

4 _____

5 _____

6 _____

7 _____

Funda

SNAKES AND LADDERS MOVEMENTS

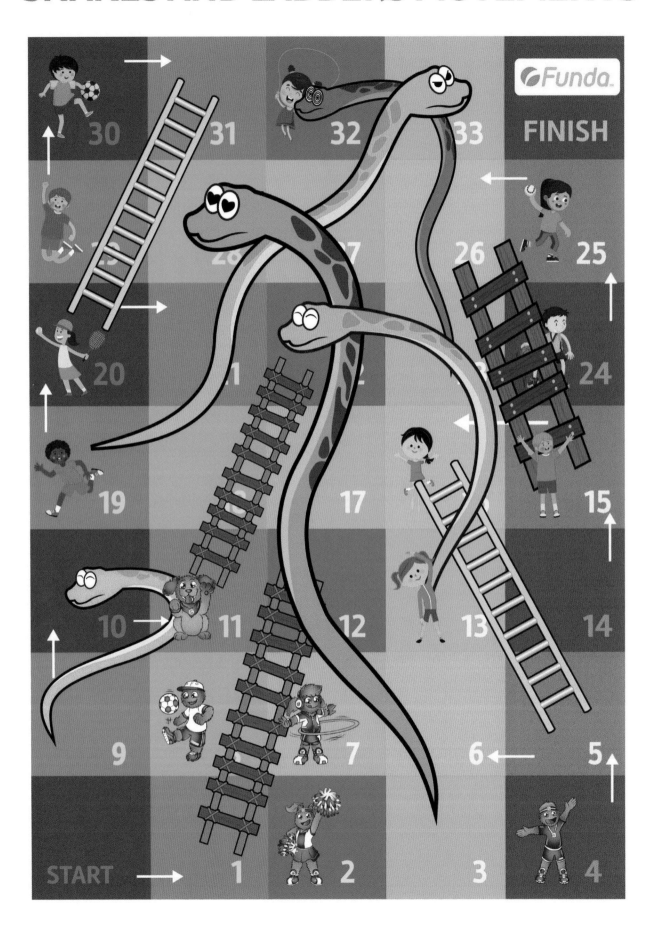

A

Adventure

a

B b

Banana

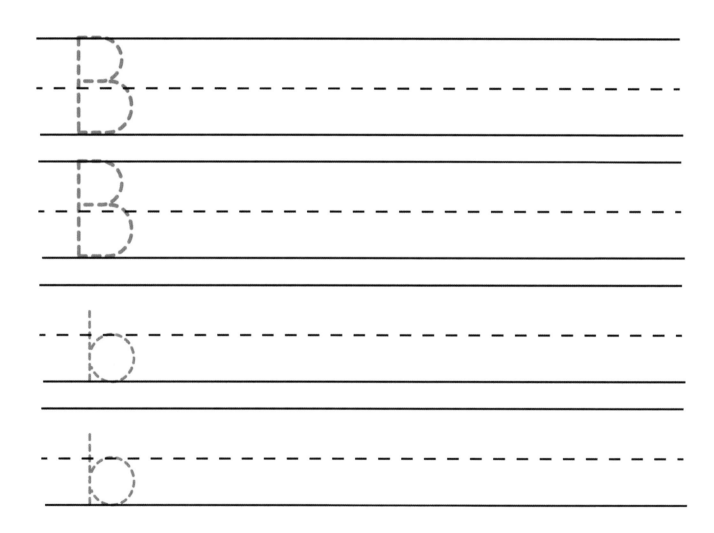

C c

Crawl like
a Crab

D d

Dog

E e

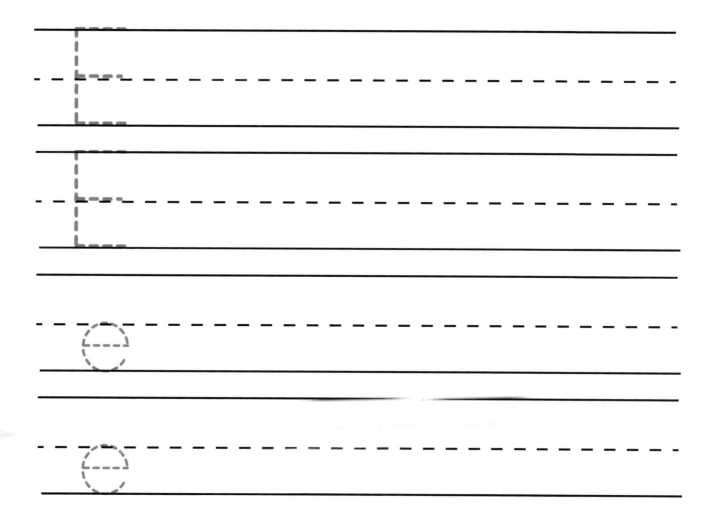

Energy

F f

FUNDA

Grapes

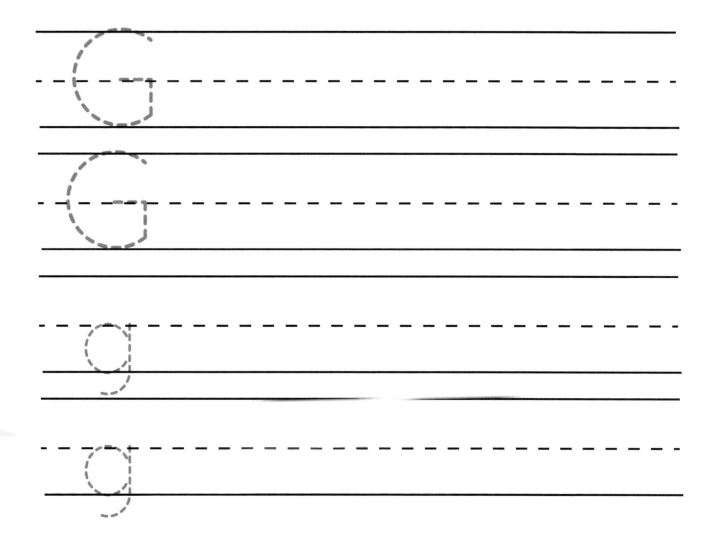

High Five

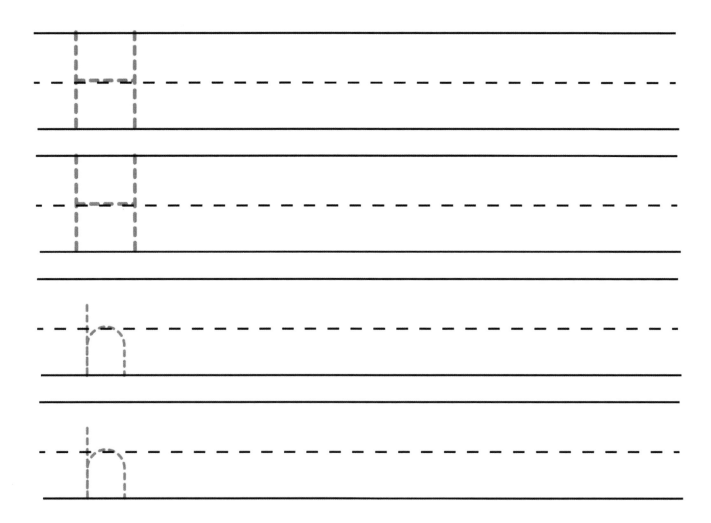

I i

Instruments

J  j

Jump

Kids

L l

Learning

M   m

March like a Toy Soldier

M

M

m

m

Nose

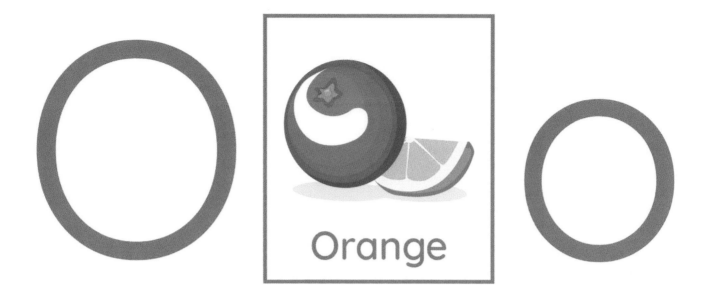

Orange

Puzzle

Quiet

R r

Race

S  S

Skip

S

S

s

s

Teddy

U  U

Unicorn

Vegetables

W  W

Winner

Xylophones

Y  y

Yoyo

Z

Zebra

Z

Active Friendly Teach **Professional**

Enthusiastic

Trust **Fun** Leader

Present Energetic

Honesty

Integrity **Role Model**

Discipline

Loyalty **Respect** **Passionate**

Humility

Caring Smart **Educate** **Creative**

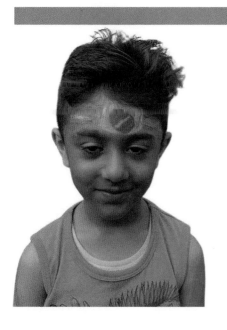

Be thankful for what you have.
Work hard for what you don't have.

My
World

Free Online Access

Thousands Of Education, Physical & Personal Development Resources, Activities For Kids Online

www.FUNDAgreatness.com

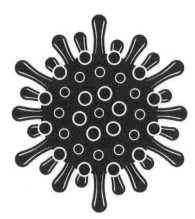

COVID-19
CORONAVIRUS

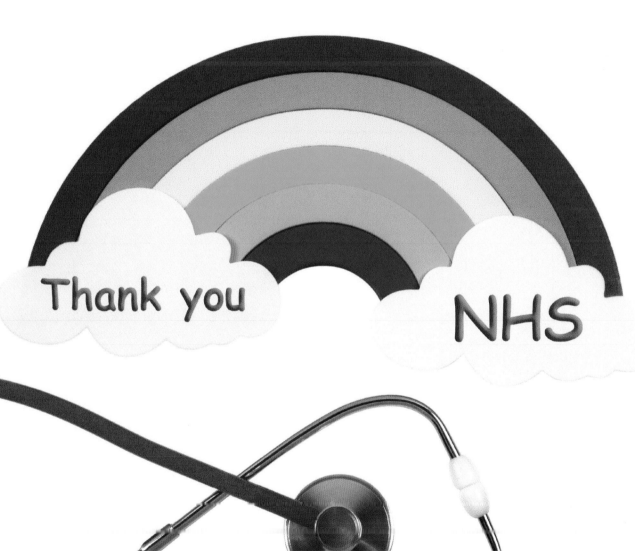

Thank you

NHS

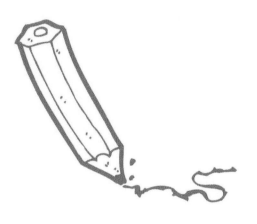

Printed in Great Britain
by Amazon